MONTCLAIR STATE UNIVERSITY

GEORGE SEGAL GALLERY

montclair.edu/segalgallery

George Segal Gallery
Montclair State University
1 Normal Avenue
Montclair, NJ 07043

Tel: 973-655-3382
Fax: 973-655-7665
montclair.edu/segalgallery

Triumph of Philippine Art

September 21 – December 15, 2013

M. Teresa Lapid Rodriguez
Curator and George Segal Gallery director

Triumph of Philippine Art

September 21 – December 15, 2013

GEORGE SEGAL GALLERY

MONTCLAIR STATE UNIVERSITY

GEORGE SEGAL
GALLERY

montclair.edu/segalgallery

1 Normal Ave., Montclair, NJ 07043

January 15 – February 23, 2014

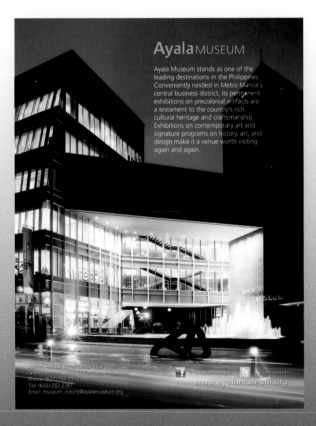

AyalaMUSEUM

Ayala Museum stands as one of the leading destinations in the Philippines. Conveniently nestled in Metro Manila's central business district, its permanent exhibitions on precolonial artifacts are a testament to the country's rich cultural heritage and craftsmanship. Exhibitions on contemporary art and signature programs on history, art, and design make it a venue worth visiting again and again.

www.ayalamuseum.org

TABLE OF CONTENTS

4   Message from Consul General Mario L. De Leon, Jr., Philippine Consulate General, New York

5   Message from Dr. Susan A. Cole, President, Montclair State University

6   Message from Ma. Elizabeth L. Gustilo, Senior Director, Arts and Culture, Ayala Museum

7   Message from Dean Daniel Gurskis, College of the Arts

8   Acknowledgments, M. Teresa Lapid Rodriguez, Director, George Segal Gallery

10   Triumph of Philippine Art by M. Teresa Lapid Rodriguez, Curator

32   Exhibition Plates

55   Exhibition Checklist

58   Appendix

60   List of Educational Events

61   Sponsors

62   Lenders

MESSAGE

The Philippine Consulate General in New York proudly joins the George Segal Gallery at Montclair State University and the Ayala Museum in the official launching of the exhibition "The Triumph of Philippine Art" focusing on Philippine Art from 1972-1986.

The exhibit features works produced during one of the most turbulent periods in Philippine history – the Martial Law Era to the EDSA People Power Revolution of 1986. The seminal events of this period led to a paradigm shift in Philippine political, economic, and sociocultural life. The art of the period mirrors the developments in these event-filled years and acts as a prism through which history and its ramifications are refracted and viewed.

The art of the period, as seen through the works of featured artists including Brenda Fajardo, Benedicto Cabrera, Elmer Borlongan, Karen Ocampo Flores, Imelda Cajipe Endaya, Christina Quisimbing Ramilo, Athena Magcase Lopez, Gregory Raymond Halili, Julie Lluch, Renan Ortiz, Pablo Baen Santos, Michael Gomez, Mark Orozco Justiniani, Buen Calubayan, Mark Salvatus, Ernest Concepcion, Leo Abaya, and Mideo Cruz, offers a glimpse of this significant period in Philippine history, the imprint of which will be felt for generations.

The Consulate General congratulates all those involved in the staging of this major exhibit under the guidance and keen eye of curator, M. Teresa Lapid Rodriguez.

Mabuhay to all the participating artists, organizers and patrons of "The Triumph of Philippine Art"!

MARIO L. DE LEON, JR.
Consul General

21 September 2013, New York

Detail from
Gregory Raymond Halili
Constellation XI, 2007

556 Fifth Avenue, New York, NY 10036
Tel No. (212)-764-1330 Fax No. (212)-764-6010 E-mail: commcen@newyorkpcg.org Website: www.newyorkpcg.org

A MESSAGE FROM PRESIDENT SUSAN A. COLE

From 1972 through the People Power Revolution of 1986, the Philippines endured a prolonged period of economic, social, and political struggle. This difficult period generated an artistic response that was rich in a wide array of forms with an astonishing breadth of styles, ranging from the subtle and symbolic to the provocative and direct.

In this exhibition, **The Triumph of Philippine Art**, a society in transition is reflected in the work of its artists. Uniquely Filipino, the art moves from themes of criticism and rebellion to those of liberation and celebration. In their search for a new national identity, the artists find inspiration in local cultures, indigenous materials, and the everyday lives of the people, a signal artistic development in a society that had been for centuries shaped by colonial rule.

I invite you to tour this exhibition of the vibrant and unique contemporary art of the Philippines in the George Segal Gallery and to take advantage of the many workshops, lectures, and presentations offered in conjunction with the exhibition.

Detail from Imelda Cajipe Endaya
Seedlings Trellis, 1982

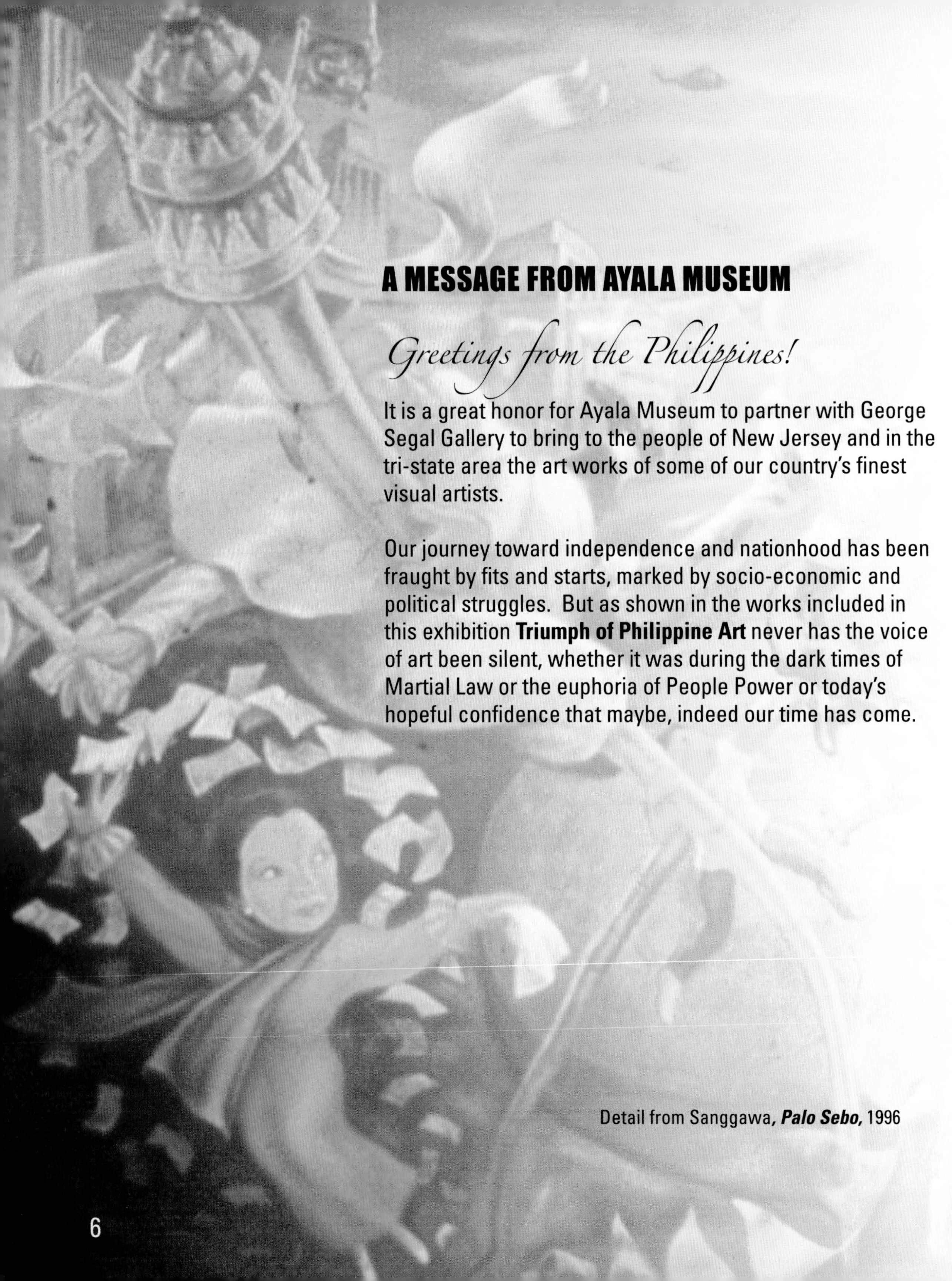

A MESSAGE FROM AYALA MUSEUM

Greetings from the Philippines!

It is a great honor for Ayala Museum to partner with George Segal Gallery to bring to the people of New Jersey and in the tri-state area the art works of some of our country's finest visual artists.

Our journey toward independence and nationhood has been fraught by fits and starts, marked by socio-economic and political struggles. But as shown in the works included in this exhibition **Triumph of Philippine Art** never has the voice of art been silent, whether it was during the dark times of Martial Law or the euphoria of People Power or today's hopeful confidence that maybe, indeed our time has come.

The Ayala Museum was established in 1967 under the auspices of Ayala Foundation as a museum of Philippine history and iconography. Today, it is one of the leading art and history museums in the Philippines, committed to disseminating and promoting awareness & understanding of Philippine art & culture. It is in this spirit that we proudly partner with George Segal Gallery on the exhibition **Triumph of Philippine Art** and wish them all the success.

Mabuhay!

Ma. Elizabeth "Mariles" L. Gustilo
Senior Director, Arts and Culture
Ayala Museum
Makati City, Philippines

Detail from Sanggawa, *Palo Sebo,* 1996

6

A MESSAGE FROM DEAN DANIEL GURSKIS

A headline in a respected Asian newspaper recently posed the question, "Are we in a golden age of Philippine art?" The article went on to take note of the dynamic art scene, the thriving gallery system, the proliferation of auction houses, and the growing international interest in the Filipino artists as indicators of the robust state of contemporary art in the Philippines.

If Philippine art is in fact in a golden age, its roots can surely be traced back to the period beginning with the institution of martial law in 1972 and concluding with the People Power Revolution of 1986. During that time, the country was beset by extremes of repression, corruption, and poverty. It is hard to imagine that those circumstances would serve to inspire, but inspire they did, giving rise to an extended period of prolific and diverse work by Philippine artists. Initially focused on resistance, the art ultimately captured the zeitgeist of a society in transition. The scope of the work on display here in the **Triumph of Philippine Art** crystalizes the truly remarkable role of art and artists in the reanimation of a nation.

We are pleased that you have joined us at the George Segal Gallery, and we hope that you enjoy this very special exhibition.

Detail from Christina Quisumbing Ramilo,
Mukhang Pera, 2010

7

Detail from Renan Ortiz,
VerseReverse, 2011

ACKNOWLEDGMENTS
BY M. TERESA LAPID RODRIGUEZ

I am happy to present and curate The Triumph of Philippine Art for Montclair State University and the general public to enjoy. As curator of the exhibition, my challenges were primarily in the careful selection of works from hundreds of Filipino and Filipino American artists' works. Two years ago when I visited the Philippines to revive my research of nearly 20 years, I was surprised to find a vibrant Philippine art community and contemporary works that are robust, diverse, and globally competitive. The pleasant surprise, I realized, is part of an inspired Philippine historical continuum of the last fifty years that explored uniquely Filipino imagery and materials. It became my focus for this exhibition. With such artistic wealth, the limitations of this exhibition became facilities, travel, and funding. This exhibition and many more Filipino and Filipino American contemporary works are worthwhile seeing for their aesthetic uniqueness, rebranding contemporary Philippine art of the 21st century.

I am grateful to Ambassador Mario L. De Leon, Vice Consul KhrystinaCorpus, and Maria Victoria Dimaculangan of the Philippine Consulate General of New York for their enthusiasm, support, and promotion of the exhibition to the Filipino and Filipino American community, and to our enthusiastic partners, Ms. Maria Elizabeth Gustilo, director, Aprille Tijam, exhibition manager, and Kenneth Esguerra, curator and conservator of the Ayala Museum, for their great help in collecting and transporting the works from Manila and in presenting the exhibition at the Ayala Museum. I am also especially grateful to former Ayala Foundation president, Victoria Pineda Garchitorena, who in 2010 visited Montclair State and encouraged my plan to present this exhibition. And to Dr. Patrick Flores and Dayang Yraola of the Vargas Museum, University of the Philippines, artists Imelda Cajipe-Endaya, Christina Quisumbing Ramilo, and Mario Fernandez for their assistance in linking me to many other talented Filipino artists. I also thank all the artists who are in the show for lending their works and generous time. Likewise, I thank other lenders—Ateneo de Manila University Art Gallery, Norman Crisologo, The Drawing Room Contemporary Art Manila and Singapore, Prof. Maria Lourdes Jacob, The Estate of Melvyn Patrick Lopez, Lynda and Stewart Resnick, Ninotchka Rosca, Tin-Aw Gallery, and the University of the Philippines Bulwagan ng Dangal.

The exhibition is complemented with meaningful educational programs for which the George Segal Gallery is indebted to the following scholars and prominent community members: writers Luis Francia and feminist Ninotchka Rosca, playwright Jorshinelle Taleon-Sonza, pianist Reynaldo Reyes, and rondallistas Del Gow, Clarita Ramos, and Flordeliza Yalong. Thanks are due as well to the Filipino American community leaders for their enthusiasm, support, and services: Zenaida Almario, Corazon Tolentino, and Madelyn Yu, and to Montclair State University's Dora Lim and Raquel Peterson.

I thank Montclair State University for its support and encouragement to present this exhibition: President Susan A. Cole, Provost Willard Gingerich, Advancement Vice President John Shannon, College of the Arts Dean Daniel Gurskis, Associate Dean Ronald Sharps, Assistant Dean Linda Davidson, the Broadcasting Department's Nick Tzanis, Patty Piroh and Brian Carter, and IT's John O'Brien for the online streaming program; Communication's Bob Gano, Randi Rosh, and Jordan Peled for proofreading all written materials, Director of Media Relations Suzanne Bronski, Stefani Whitehouse for graphic design, Professor David Witten and Martha Learner for concert programs, Steve Shapiro for organizing a list of Sprague Library books relating to the Philippines; technical support from the College of the Arts' Marie Sparks, Gene Lotito, and Kilolo Kumanyika, and to Dr. Elizabeth Valdes del Alamo of the Art and Design Department; the Montclair State University Filipino American Student Association (MUFASA), especially to Aissa Sunga, former vice president, and Angelo Bautista, current president. I also thank our talented consultants, Gail Shube, graphic designer, and Erika Bleiberg, media outreach, who have worked hard on the graphic design and marketing of the exhibition. And my dedicated staff, education coordinator Carol Del Guidice, registrarial assistant Coral Payano, and exhibition designer Anthony Louis Rodriguez, who have worked patiently with me in producing this challenging exhibition.

Finally, I am grateful to the following sponsors whose support made this exhibition possible: The New Jersey State Council on the Arts, John McMullen Family Foundation, University of the Philippines Alumni Association, NJ, V. C. Igarta Arts Center, Norbert and Elizabeth Wirsching, Advent Consulting Associates, Inc., Millenia of Philippine Art, Inc., Tess Aguilar, Rolly and Zeny Almario, Fil-am Pag-asa Club of UMDNJ, Del Gow, Flordeliza Yalong, Maureen Promin, Cora Crisostomo Tolentino, and Myrna Sangil Vergara. Thanks also go to the George Segal Gallery advisory board for keeping our Art Connections fundraiser vibrant and a vital support to our exhibitions

My heartfelt thanks to everyone. Enjoy the exhibition!

Triumph of Philippine Art

By M. Teresa Lapid Rodriguez

ART REFLECTS THE COUNTRY'S HISTORY

Origin Of Philippine Imagery

The Philippines is an archipelago located in Southeast Asia. A nation with over 7,000 islands, its existence of over 4,000 years includes in its history a little-known civilization that was said to have flourished between the fifth and the tenth centuries A.D.[1] Among its earliest available signs of culture are recently discovered gold treasures of Vedic Hindu-Buddhist influence dating back to the ninth century. These were found in burial sites in many parts of the country. Archaeologist Peter Bellwood is convinced that the artifacts were locally produced because of evidence of widespread use and his discovery of an ancient goldsmith shop in the region. Among the gold artifacts discovered is a ***kinnari*** vessel (Fig. 1, front and back) unearthed in Surigao del Sur, southern Philippines, now in the Ayala Museum collection, that provides a glimpse of early Philippine imagery.[2] A ***kinnari*** is a mythic half-woman/half-bird deity believed to have the power to enlighten and graced with beauty and musical ability. The myth originated in India.

The elegant vessel renders a human female head and torso with classic Malay facial features of a wide forehead, wide elongated eyes, high cheekbones and striated hair bundled up in the back that is secured with a piece of jewelry and ending in a knot at the base. The torso is that of a female while the lower body is that of a bird with suggestions of feathers incised on it.

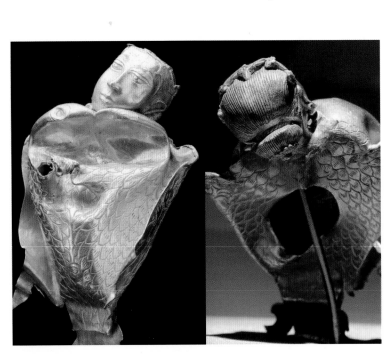

*Fig. 1, **Kinnari Vessel** (front and back) unearthed in Surigao del Sur, southern Philippines, Ca. 10th-13th century, 12 x 7.5 cm., Ayala Museum Collection*

Many more artifacts display a rich array of jewelry and wearable accessories providing clues to pre-Hispanic Philippine designs. Explorers from southern China, who visited the country in 900 A.D., and Arab traders, who brought in Islam in the 14th century, also influenced Philippine imagery subtly, appearing in some contemporary art of the Philippines. But it is with the coming of Spain in the 16th century that imagery was thoroughly fashioned to suit colonial taste over a 300-year period beginning with the initial introduction of European religious images, which supplanted earlier images.

The year 1521 marks the entry of Spain into the Philippines, naming it after its king, Philip II. Captain General Ferdinand Magellan, a Portuguese sailing for Spain who died during his discovery visit to the Philippines in the fatal duel with Cebu Island's chieftain, Lapu-lapu, nevertheless succeeded in planting the seed of Christianity in the land. The actual occupation of the country began in 1565 under the command of Captain General Miguel Lopez de Legaspi by way of the Visayan Islands. By 1567 he reached and occupied Manila, then the biggest trading and Islamic culture center in the islands. Painting was introduced by Roman Catholic priests to satisfy the need for religious images in the churches, clearly indicating they were there to stay. Flemish religious images were copied by local artisans under the supervision of friars. The succeeding two centuries generated controlled colonial art. Filipino artists did not sign their works until the secularization of art in early 19th century when relative artistic freedom was possible. This freedom found an expression in portraiture that was patronized by the *Ilustrados*, educated Filipino middle-class patrons who rose up as a distinctive social class in the 19th century.

A major artistic breakthrough occurs at the 1884 *Exposición General de Bellas Artes*, Madrid, Spain, where the gold and silver medals were won by *ilustrado* artists Juan Luna for his oil painting, *Spoliarium,* and Felix Resurreccion Hidalgo for his oil painting of *Las Cristianas Expuestas al Populacho (The Christian Virgins Exposed to the Populace)*. Luna's *Spoliarium* (160 in x 280 inches) now in the National Museum of the Philippines, painted in the neoclassical style prevalent during the period, is a scene of a fallen gladiator inhumanly treated in a chamber of an ancient Roman coliseum called a *spoliarium*. The painting is electrifying in content and execution. Luna, a member of the Philippine Reform Movement, relates the painting to the Philippine colonial predicament as captive of Spain. A visual camouflage such as this is a clever device to conceal his real intent of denouncing colonial oppression.

Double-meaning imagery was common in the colonial art of the Philippines. The late 19th century saw the escalation of Filipino resistance and led to a Filipino revolution against Spain in 1896, the catalyst being a series of executions of Filipinos—three Filipino priests accused of sedition (Gomez, Burgos and Zamora) and the execution of Dr. Jose Rizal for his seditious book, *Noli Me Tangere (Touch Me Not)*. The events sparked the patriotism and bravery of labor leader Andres Bonifacio, founder of the underground armed resistance, *Kataastaasang, Kagalang-galangang, Katipunan ng mga Anak ng Bayan* (KKK, literally meaning Supreme and Venerable Society of the Children of the Nation). Immediately after its loss in the Filipino-Spanish war, the Spanish government

"Double-meaning imagery was common in the colonial art of the Philippines."

relinquished the country to the United States as war remuneration. Filipino war with the U.S. immediately ensued with a Filipino loss at the turn of the 20th century, leaving the country under U.S. colonial rule for 46 years.

*I*t was during the American colonial period (1898–1946) that Filipinized visual expression developed in the hands of a visionary of beauty, Fernando Amorsolo, who introduced his concept of an ideal Philippine beauty as described below by Amorsolo's biographer, Dr. Rodolfo Paras-Perez:

> *… one with a rounded face, not of oval type often presented to us in newspapers and magazine illustrations. The eyes should be exceptionally lively, not the dreamy, sleepy type that characterizes the Mongolian. The nose should be of the blunt form but firm and strongly marked. The mouth plays a very important part in the determination of a beautiful face. The ideal Filipina beauty should have a sensuous mouth, not the type of the pouting mouth of the early days…. So the ideal Filipina beauty should not necessarily be white complexioned, nor of the dark brown color of the typical Malayan, but of the clear skin or flesh colored type which we often witness when we meet a blushing girl.[3]*

In contrast to the world's measure of beauty, Venus de Milo, Amorsolo set his ideal Filipina beauty on a farm as a farm worker. He is, in fact, well-loved for his works that had mass appeal due to their pastoral, idealized, and slightly romantic nature featuring agrarian landscapes and local festivities surrounded by inviting local blossoms, fruits and delicacies. These heart-warming visions are either signs of relative peace or escapism into an idealized world.

Modern Art and the International Style

*F*ernando Amorsolo's legacy is challenged by the arrival of architect/painter Victorio Edades in 1928 from the West Coast of the United States who brought with him modernist principles learned from the University of Washington. Expounding on the principles of expressionism, he states that art should be a reflection of the artist's personal experience and emotions, and that distortion should be allowed in its formal construction appropriately to express the experiences and emotions. Diametrically opposing the academic style of Amorsolo, Edades saw the need for a national art based on reality and not on idealism. He introduced mural art in public places for mass access with the help of his assistants, Carlos Francisco and Galo Ocampo. Inspiration came from the works of Mexicans Diego Rivera, Rufino Tamayo, and Clemente Orozco, whom Edades had seen in his travels.

He developed a group of 13 artists simply called **13 Moderns,** who established visual expression on their own, unlike expressionism in its true sense, but one that broke away from the academic style of Luna, Hidalgo, and the Amorsolo school. The exponents of the new movement, who called themselves neo-realists, were Vicente Manansala, Hernando Ocampo, Romeo Tabuena, Victor Oteyza, Ramon Estella, and Cesar Legaspi,[4] who created images that bear resemblance to cubism due to linear application but with mesmerizing translucence and grace even in hard-edged manifestations. At times compared to cubist Pablo Picasso and Georges Braque, whose missions were to break away from the established figurative format, especially rejecting the Renaissance principles, these Filipino works are simply different in principle but unique in that sense. An example of such work is Vicente Manansala's **Pila sa Bigas** (Fig. 2, literally **Rice Rationing Line)**. Edades, who introduced modern principles in art, has been honored with the title of father of Philippine modern art. Nevertheless, art critic Leonides Benesa speaks of the neo-realists' works as a true iconoclastic breakthrough that allowed Philippine art to

Fig. 2, Vicente Manansala,
Pila Sa Bigas
1980, Oil on canvas, 54 x 84 inches
Paulino and Hetty Que Collection
Photo credit: Ayala Museum.

move forward to another dimension. The 1960s generation of artists pushed figurative imagery aside, adhering to abstraction and non-objective art, which dominated the mainstream international style in the 1950s where purely formalistic applications upheld the principle of art for art's sake. Philippine art succeeded in promoting this purely formalistic approach to art as exemplified in the works of talented Professor Jose Joya. In the long run, however, the trend took its toll on its alienating effect to society. The late 1960s and 1970s see a looming restless society on the brink of civil war.

Struggle for National Identity

Only 26 years after the 1946 Philippine independence from the U.S., history would repeat itself, not by another colonizer but by a dictator. Proclamation No. 1081 gave Philippine president Ferdinand Marcos the authority to declare martial law on September 21, 1972, a move that took away people's basic rights and in turn took away people's trust in the government. This brought back memories of the 19th-century heroism, rousing indignation and organized actions in colleges and universities where activism and student mass movements took roots.

In visual art, abstract and non-objective art along with the principles of art for art's sake, were rejected in favor of figurative expressionism, where the abuses of military rule were laid out in political paintings and sculptures. Political art is reborn with a vengeance. Artistic content of works not only covered the immediate political issues and the abusive regime but also criticized social, economic and religious problems besetting the country. The marginalized—women, children, farmers, laborers and the ethnic minorities—along with human rights violations were themes that proliferated in the art community. The artists of this period put the society itself on trial on their canvases.

Deemed inappropriate by law, artistic content of this kind could easily cause an artist to be incarcerated during martial law in the Philippines. An example is a 1975, 24 x 36 inch oil on canvas painting entitled *PSR1* (Fig. 3),[5] an attempt to visually interpret the book *Philippine Social Revolution* written in 1964 by political exile Jose Maria Sison. The work, now lost, depicts burning farmlands on the top left and factories on the right symbolizing abusive practices in these regions. An advancing mass of people of all classes populate the canvas. The central figure, a glorified albeit melancholy mother wearing the Philippine flag and nursing her infant on the right as her toddler stands half-naked on the left, is an allegory of matriarchal Philippines contemplating a bleak future of her people.

Further artistic initiatives motivated local research of the Filipino culture and search for and use of local non-traditional materials such as tarot cards, *sawali* (interleaved bamboo mats used as walls for nipa huts [indigenous Philippine housing]), blood, religious images, glass, debris, polymer clay, toilet paper, mylar, bullet casings, digital images, linoleum, cultured pearl, nacreous clamshell, etc., which undoubtedly were efforts to link Filipino art to its environment and culture, a dramatic departure from the international style. Exponents of this initiative are "21st century" BenCab, Brenda Fajardo, Imelda Cajipe-Endaya, Mideo Cruz, Mark Salvatus, Christina Quisumbing Ramilo, Gregory Raymond Halili, Racquel DeLoyola, Buen Calubayan, Mark Orozco Justiniani, Leo Abaya, Renan Ortiz and Michael Geronimo Rodriguez

Fig. 3, M. Teresa Lapid Rodriguez, *PSR1*, 1975, oil on canvas, 36 x 24 in., Courtesy of the artist

"In visual art, abstract and non-objective art along with the principles of art for art's sake, were rejected in favor of figurative expressionism"

Gomez, whose works are represented in this exhibition. Those whose art were of traditional materials articulated gut-wrenching imagery such as, "late 20th century" BenCab, Julie Lluch and Athena Santos Magcase-Lopez. Research of the history, local culture, and the environment generated local imagery. That the Philippines is primitive, feudal and modern all at once has been turned into an artistic advantage in furthering distinctive imagery and unique personality to contemporary Philippine art. Ernest Concepcion and "21st century" Mark Orozco Justiniani, who maintains dual Philippine/U.S. citizenship, are among those paving the way to the global world. The period is fraught with questions, and the need-to-know attitude led to the rebranding of Filipinos and Filipino art by Filipinos and Filipino artists.

A long-embattled quest for identity was reached in the years following a phenomenal people-power movement of 1986 that ousted a brilliant dictator by sheer numbers of people of all classes marching in millions, denouncing the regime. The extraordinary restraint exercised, leaving no one harmed, had been called a miracle. But it must be the extraordinary human spirit that Filipinos found in themselves to stand above violence. Certainly, this is a milestone achieved on many levels and a triumph in Philippine Art.

*P*olitical art reborn in the decades of the 1960s, 1970s, and 1980s is radical, at times visually combative, structured and guided by manifestos. Below is a sample manifesto from a group of social realists founded in 1976.[6]

Kaisahan (Solidarity) Declaration of Principles

We, the artists of KAISAHAN, commit ourselves to the search for national identity.

We believe that national identity is not to be found in a nostalgic love of the past or an idealized view of our traditions and our history. It cannot be achieved by using the common symbols of our national experience without understanding the reality that lies within them. We recognize that national identity, if it is to be more than lip service or an excuse for personal status seeking, should be firmly based on the present social realities and a critical assessment of our historical past so that we may trace the roots of these realities.

We shall therefore develop an art that reflects the true conditions and problems in our society.

This means, first of all, that we must break away from the western-oriented culture that tends to maintain the Filipino people's dependence on foreign tastes and foreign ways that are incompatible with their genuine interests. We reject this culture in so far as it perpetuates values, habits and attitudes that do not serve the people's welfare, but draw from it whatever is useful to their actual needs.

We shall therefore move away from the uncritical acceptance of western models, from the slavish imitation of western forms that have no connection to our national life, from the preoccupation with western trends that do not reflect the process of our development.

We realize that our search will be meaningless [if] it does not become a collective experience, an experience that is understood by the broadest number of people. In its beginning, art was not the isolated act that it is now: it was as necessary, as integral, a part of the people's lives as the knowledge of when to plant.

For us therefore, the question "for whom is art?" is a crucial and significant one. And our experiences lead us the answer that art is for the masses. It must not exist simply for the pleasure of the few who can afford it. It must not degenerate into the pastime of the few cultists.

(The three-page manifesto, courtesy of one of its founders, Pablo Baen-Santos,[7] is printed in full in the appendix of the catalogue.)

The Exhibition

The works in this exhibition were selected to demonstrate groundbreaking developments from the early 1970s to the present that led to the establishment of distinctive and unique imagery in Philippine contemporary art, achieved by way of figurative expressionism, social realism and conceptual art. The selections were guided by examples of innovations in content, form and material, exquisite quality of execution, poignant messages or clever disposition.

Figurative Expressionism and Social Realism

Figurative expressionism is an outgrowth of abstract expressionism delivered in figurative format. In mainstream art of the late 19th century to the mid-20th century, it is simply a personal experience imbued with deep emotions, such as the works of Vincent Van Gogh, Edvard Munch, and Willem DeKooning. It is a cry of human anguish typically displaying highly charged narrative of a situation in turmoil. Figurative expressionism is personal, individualistic and unstructured, with no goal other than to express anguish, unlike the structured and goal-oriented social realism. Whereas social realism has a distinct beginning and ending in a society that is usually facing oppression, figurative expressionism simply appears and disappears in the art scene. While figurative expressionism is relegated to mannerism, and social realism is a style, both art forms could coexist in the community sometimes with no obvious distinguishing difference from each other due to their strong appeal to the emotion.

*Fig. 4, Benedicto Cabrera, **From Hillman to Sergeant**, 1978, 3-color plate etching, 21 x 24 in., Collection of the artist*

An early proponent of figurative expressionism in the Philippines is National Artist **BenCab** (Benedicto Reyes Cabrera), whose figurative works of the 1970s produced thought-provoking images of injustice and violence during the martial law period. An example is his 1975 etching/aquatint entitled ***1081,*** referencing the Martial Law Proclamation No. 1081 (Pl. 1), which features an imposing figure of a soldier, back turned to the viewer, in full military gear, dominating the center of the work standing on top of lifeless bodies of Filipinos. On the top left is the boss, with the upper half of his face cropped but its lower half unmistakably that of President Ferdinand Marcos, clenched fist denoting his power as commander-in-chief of the military. Face cropping is apparently a device BenCab effectively introduced to Philippine art,[8] an attention-grabbing, emotionally charged element common to figurative expressionism. On the top right are street protesters wielding banners, including one of the 19th-century resistance banners of the **Katipunan** (KKK) partially hidden, and an iconic papier-mâché bust of Uncle Sam representing the United States' support of the regime.

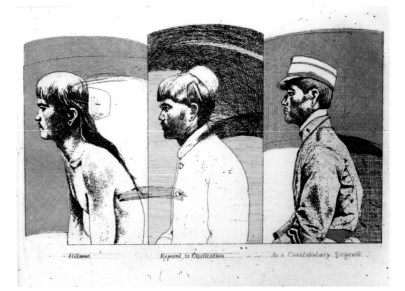

Another etching /aquatint, dated 1978 and titled **From Hillman to Sergeant** (Fig. 4), features a triptych profile of a young man in three progressive stages of development. Captioned, "Hillman," the first profile is a generalized feature of a young **Ifugao**[9] tribesman from the northern Cordillera region of the Philippines wearing a small woven grass hat on the lower back of his head partially covering long thick black hair, the naked upper torso exposing slightly drooping shoulders and slightly bent back. The second image, captioned "Exposed to Civilization," features the same young man now wearing a high-collared coat, shortened hair, and the same hat set higher on the head. The third image, labeled "As a Constabulary Sergeant," features the man in military attire no longer naïve but stern-faced, his hair in a military cut, and wearing a hat matching his military coat. Judging from his uniform another player is identified—

communist Red China—that the 1970s student movement idealized. BenCab's attention to detail is quite discerning showing careful transformation of one image to the next, descriptive outfits, hair styles, and backgrounds of verdant green representing minimalized lush-mountain, gradually transforming into an ambivalent black and red background in the second image and simply red in the third image. Clever is the ultimate word to describe this work that summarized the complexity of Philippine Martial Law in one small work. This work, which seems to be a study, appears as a central piece in a much bigger composition entitled *Invaders and Resisters*, a 1980 acrylic on paper.

Fig. 5, Benedicto Cabrera, Marlboro Country, 1975, etching aquatint, 23 x 21 in., Collection of the artist

His *Marlboro Country* (Fig. 5), another etching and aquatint, features a woman, back turned to the viewer, contemplating a billboard advertisement of the cigarette, implying a longing for the American dream. BenCab has been praised for his exceptional draftsmanship, and in this work the skill reveals in the delicate treatment of fabric texture and folds enveloping the figure. "[The fabric folds'] fascination for me lies in the beauty of their simplicity and delicateness,"[10] he is quoted as commenting on the exquisite quality of this etching. The stylized clouds floating in the background are Asian in construction. In contrast, *O.T. in Chicago*, representing a suited, educated and contented Filipino-American immigrant whose demeanor

nevertheless subtly conveys a pragmatic, melancholy, matter-of-fact existence. Stylistically, the artist's capability to convey complex psychology in visual terms could only be attributed to his impeccable command of draftsmanship.

Pablo Baen Santos is a front runner of social realism. In 1976, he organized the first social realist group called *Kaisahan* (Solidarity) for the purpose of affecting social change. Typical of his works are criticisms of the oppressive society in content and radical in format similar to the Mexican muralists of the 1930s, in particular Jose Clemente Orozco, whose thick brush strokes are as aggressive as his messages. Santos's critical themes send shock waves of raw pain or anger as in *Krista*, a 1984 painting of a woman gagged with barbed wire on her mouth, hands bound with duct tape, her clenched fists denoting defiance. Behind her is the Philippine flag signifying her allegiance to the nation. The work is made complex by multi-layered symbolism playing all at once—as motherland suppressed, defiance as a symbol of nationalism, and as a sacrificial lamb with a mission to redeem her people. His works are not limited to displeasure with the government but also cover the ills and hypocrisy in the society. In *Labor and Monkey Business* (Pl. 2), a 2010 oil on canvas, the theme focuses on the danger laborers face daily on the job, amplified quite expressively through the technique of foreshortened figures and building elements. Santos has a following of many artists who cover many aspects of social injustice and political corruption. Social realism in the Philippines still rages but has taken a different format in the 21st century in the hands of the next generation. Some works are reviewed in the following pages.

"Santos has a following of many artists who cover many aspects of social injustice and political corruption"

U.S.– based **Athena Santos Magcase-Lopez** presents a deep personal message in her ***Awit ng Isang Ina*** (Fig. 6, translated by the artist as ***Song of Motherland*** [literally, ***Song of a Mother***]), showing a real-life story of a pregnant political activist family member who was incarcerated and consequently delivered her

Fig. 6, Athena Magcase-Lopez,
Awit Ng Isang Ina
(Song of the Motherland), *1986,*
oil on canvas, 30 x 46 in.,
Courtesy of The Estate of Melvyn
Patrick Lopez

baby in prison. The background wall marked in red militant slogans partially cropped but readable—IMPERYALISTA—scribbled names of victims of martial law, and ominous shadows of jail bars cast on the wall just behind a defiant young mother all work together in heightening a chilling scene. The work is also inspired by a poem made into a song composed by the artist's husband, Melvyn, who narrowly missed death during his martial law activism. The poem appeals to his wife "to ensure the future of [our] children by taking an active role in changing [your] political landscape."[11] Even more complex is another work, ***Sumungaw na Liwanag*** (Pl. 3, ***A Ray of Hope***), done after the assassination of Senator Ninoy Aquino, whose death

provoked the People Power Movement of 1986 and the eventual ouster of President Ferdinand Marcos. Lopez's psychologically complex themes maintain internal restrained power. A teary-eyed monumentalized child in jail injects an element of surprise that defies logic. Juxtaposing innocence with mature restraint in the child's eyes and the shadowy jail cell bars surrounding the child terminates in a slightly open door, creating further twists in the narrative scene. The title and jail cell provide opposite emotions, indicating the ambivalence of life in the Philippines at that time and perhaps in the artist's heart and judgment.

Feminism

Julie Lluch, a ceramist who elevated her humble art material, Philippine red clay, exposes a deep issue of gender inequality towards women, who are made prisoners by their very role in society as nurturing mothers and submissive wives unable to participate outside of this stereotype because of their gender. To defy it demeans them as outcasts of society. For Julie Lluch the demeaning existence became a challenge when upon entering marriage and family life she encountered severely challenging gender biases and succumbed to a nervous breakdown. A strong self-made artist, she redeemed herself through her artistic expressions in clay that are now models of feminist art in the Philippines. *Philippine Gothic* (Pl. 4), a 1984 ceramic triumvirate of a husband, a wife, and a dog, presents a husband made powerful by the society's perception of him as the provider, the leader, the hero and unfortunately in some cases, a dictator of his household. On the other hand, the wife made submissive by her role as the domestic nurturer immerses herself in depression. Interestingly, between them the artist sets a dog with its attribute of loyalty foreshadowing the relationship's future. Lluch says,

> "For a woman to demand rights for her country is meddling in men's affairs; for her to demand rights for sex and class is vulgarity…. The woman who expresses unhappiness, dissatisfaction and anger must be to some extent maladjusted to the world, or to put it simply: neurotic."[12]

Liberating herself through art, she gains fame and notoriety by directly confronting sexism in society using cacti as motifs to represent yoni, phallus and hearts of thorns. Lluch's realistic works are flavored with wit and baroque gusto.

Gender inequality is in fact a world issue still plaguing many cultures of the world. In the Philippines, the marginalization of women began during the colonial times. Instances of resistance are tracked through women's organizations such as the Women's Masonic Lodge, established in 1883 by Rosario Villaruel, Trinidad and Josefa Rizal, Marina Dizon, and Romualda Lanuza, and in 1905 the Asociacion Feminista Filipina.[13] In 2005 a centennial celebration was marked by Proclamation No. 622, signed by President Gloria Macapagal Arroyo, symbolically cementing the rights of Filipino women.

Brenda Fajardo takes us back in history to the ancient magical world of the *Babaylan,* a female-dominated group believed to be empowered with special gifts of a metaphysical nature and respected as intermediaries in community affairs. They were said to have had equal rights with men in business, politics and spiritual matters. Famous for her use of mystical iconography, Fajardo features *Babaylan* power in her mythic world of tarot (Fig. 7). In the series called *Baraha ng Buhay Pilipino: Walang Katapusang Naghalo* and *Balat sa Tinalupan,* (Pl. 5, *Playing Cards of Filipino Life: Never Ending Chaos*), her tarot cards circle around a world with no boundaries, a timeless world that is a stage whose characters are members of the society playing their parts under a wheel of fate (*Gulong ng Kapalaran*)—the king (*Sultan*), angel of death (*Kamatayan*), the horseman (*Kabalyero*), justice (*Katarungan*), soldier (*Kawal*), courage (*Katatagan*) and Judgement Day (*Paghuhukom*)—and determine the fate of the central scene of a society in

Fig. 7, Brenda Fajardo,
Tarot Card Series 7,
acrylic on paper, 21 x 28 in.,
Collection of Ninotchka Rosca
Photo credit: Anthony Louis Rodriguez

turmoil. The iconic sun of the Philippine flag is the sole witness. Fajardo's multi-faceted background—a BA in agriculture, MA in Art Education at the University of Wisconsin, PhD in Philippine Studies, graphic artist, painter, theater set designer, actress—enables her to create an art form that is versatile and flexible where she makes her views on many aspects of Filipino life transparent. A bonus for feminism, Justice and Courage are represented by women, **Babaylan** attributes indeed. Deep in content, original in format, naïve in style, brave in the use of metaphysics, the series is uniquely Filipino.

Imelda Cajipe Endaya, a feminist at heart who co-founded, with Brenda Fajardo, a feminist group called **Kababaihan sa Sining at Bagong Sibol na Kamalaya,** (Women in the Arts Planting New Seeds of Consciousness) (acronym KASIBULAN [Germination]), takes her feminism to a more democratic level of the family unit, where the woman as the ultimate victim subconsciously carries her burden for the family. The man is part of it also, a victim caught in a vicious cycle of basic relationships, as demonstrated in **Seedlings Trellis** (Fig. 8). This is a powerful painting, packed with iconographic symbols—mother and child vs father, the disjointed capiz (nacreous clam shell) windows symbolizing the Philippines, the banana plant that is chopped after bearing fruits as a subservient woman's destiny, and the portentous energy running throughout the household,

society's perpetuation of institutional violence not only towards women but indirectly to the family unit. In the 1985 painting entitled **Inay Ineng Kalayaan ay Inyo Rin** (Pl. 6, **Mother, This Freedom is Yours, Too**), an enlightened daughter prepares her mother for an impending societal change. Surrounding the painting's surface is delicate lace, epitomizing the fragile female persona as well as fragile times of a country on the verge of civil war. It also technically texturizes, connects and unifies the elements in the painting surface. Endaya's use of **sawali** (woven bamboo strip mats), a material used in humble nipa (grass) huts in the Philippine countryside, instantly identifies the work of Filipino origin. She says of this painting, "these were the years when I was such an isolated wife and mother who longed to have a more social/political role in my art. I always have to budget basic family needs before I can buy my paints, so when the budget is low I simply use day-to-day domestic objects within my reach.... I used actual bamboo mat windows and the nipa leaves, which were roofing materials I took from my garden hut...."[14]

Fig. 8, *Imelda Cajipe Endaya,*
Seedlings Trellis, 1982,
oil on canvas, 91.5 cm x 122 cm,
Collection of Sue Cannon

Karen Ocampo Flores, who may be better known for her collaborative murals, is also a feminist who articulates her feminist ideas in her individual paintings. The 2006 acrylic on canvas, **A Line of History** (Pl. 7), depicts a woman's quandary in colonial Philippines from a non-Catholic tribal woman to a church devotee working on her salvation. Strewn around the canvas are various symbols of Spanish occupation icons distinctly separating the Spanish from the Filipino, reflecting the racial segregation during Spanish times. Unusual, however, are the moths and butterflies populating the sky like a WWII airstrike. On closer look they bear much deeper meaning(s), giving mythological credence as nature's messengers.

The Filipino national hero, Dr. Jose Rizal, in his 1884 speech, compared the transformation of a cocoon into a butterfly to a dawning new free Philippines. Butterflies are seen as creatures of daylight offering new hope. On the other hand,

moths are seen in many cultures as creatures of the night circling the light that eventually kills them.

On the contrary, Mexican writer Carlos Castaneda in his **Tales of Power** wrote of the moth as a prophetic bearer of the future. At the bottom of the canvas is a serpentine dragon that in Asian mythology symbolizes wisdom and longevity. Underneath this scene is a fully stretched Philippine flag cleverly veiled, the blue half over the red indicating a period of peace. In her 2008 painting **A View of the World** (**Ang Mundo**) Flores sets her woman on top of the world in a swimsuit, red caped and holding a scepter as a title holder in a beauty pageant. Sarcasm appears to be Flores' way of delivering her messages quite clearly.

*T*he first art collaborative group she helped form is **Sanggawa** (**One Work**), whose productions result from a group effort that supports two ground rules— no one dominates the other, and no style surpasses

the other. Remarkably, personal stylistic signatures are undetectable on these gigantic mural formats like the **Palo Sebo** (Fig. 9), which is based on a Filipino town square contest normally played in town **fiestas.** In

Fig. 9, *Sanggawa*, **Palo Sebo**, *1996, oil on canvas*

this case it is set in the tone of a political race where political figures race to the top of slippery bamboo poles. President Fidel Ramos and Cardinal Jaime Sin climb neck and neck; witnesses below are former First Lady Imelda Marcos surrounded by money, past President Corazon Aquino surrounded with church devotional items, and not far behind, future President

Gloria Macapagal Arroyo leaning on a bamboo shoot. The deceased Ferdinand Marcos's image still influences the society in a flyer, feminism struggling, and families breaking up are all trapped or sucked

in a vortex representing the Philippine society of the 1990s. The work, too large to travel, is brilliant in concept and execution, but, unfortunately, will not be in the exhibition. This work is a collaborative production of five artists including Karen Ocampo Flores, Elmer Burlongan, Mark Justiniani, Federico Seivert and Joy Mallari.

A New Generation in the 21st Century

At the turn of the 21st century the Philippines is still in turmoil, with an unpopular administration under Gloria Macapagal Arroyo. The economy, wracked with severe unemployment, forces Filipinos to seek work outside the country. Remittances sent to the families in the Philippines by overseas workers (OFW) have strengthened the country's economy quite significantly, effecting a phenomenal rise in the gross domestic product (GDP).

However, the Philippine diaspora soon reveals the negative effects of exporting labor outside the country: the brain drain and the splitting of families apart are seen as clear threats to society. Government corruption persists, including control of the government by a few political dynasties, viewed by some as the root cause of corruption. Ironically, this situation is perpetrated through the corruption of the democratic process of suffrage by widespread vote buying in the poorest sectors of society, making this sacred right a farce. Although the revised 1987 constitution included a ban on political dynasties, the practice continues because the lawmakers are themselves members of

political dynasties. A 2007–2010 survey showed that more than 75 percent of the country's lawmakers and members of government are members of political dynasties.[15]

This fact has not escaped the young self-made artist/lawyer, **Michael Geronimo Rodriguez Gomez,** who memorialized the travesties of Philippine politics in his caricatured sculptures. In ***Duplicity Multiplicity*** (Pl. 8), a polymer clay done in 2013, he presents a grandfather, father and son all serving in government as lawmakers. And in ***Botokabajan*** (Fig. 10, a colloquial expression meaning "are you in favor?"), his monumental voter in a red clown suit is depicted as being entertained by a "belittled" political candidate standing on a yellow ballot box begging for a vote. Behind the clown are obscure gray little figures representing the masses. Sarcasm is sometimes good. Gomez's style is influenced by his passion as a kid for comics of the superhero type, like Superman and Spider-Man, defenders of the community. His meticulous attention to details such as the articulation of little human figures and architectural intricacies are enhancing surprises to his compositions. He says of these works, "My artwork is the convergence of my being a lawyer, an idealist, and a Filipino. Lawyers are trained to properly identify the facts of a case, the legal issues involved, and the expected outcome or resolution based on these facts and issues. These are the same skills which I try to apply in my artwork."[16]

*Fig. 10, Michael Geronimo R. Gomez, **Botokabajan**, 2012, mixed (polymer clay, wood, terra cotta clay, cement, paper), 8 x 5 x 5 in., courtesy of Michael Geronimo R. Gomez*

"...the Philippine diaspora soon reveals the negative effects of exporting labor outside the country: the brain drain and the splitting of families apart are seen as clear threats to society."

ew Jerseyan **Gregory Raymond Halili** has become famous for his miniature works as small as one inch square, and in this exhibition he has the most charming, peaceful and elegant view of the world. Highly skilled with particular focus on the Philippines, Halili selects Philippine natural resources as his materials and painstakingly paints in large series, such as one hundred Philippine butterflies (Fig. 11), one hundred tribes, and

Fig. 11, Gregory Raymond Halili, ***Constellation XI***, 2007, watercolor on paper, 10 x 10 in., courtesy of Gregory Raymond Halili

lately, expressive eyes referencing a cultural icon, **Mater Dolorosa**, the grieving Virgin Mary of the Passion of Christ, superbly painted on nacreous clamshell entitled **Sorrow I**, (Pl. 9). Halili says of his work, "Nostalgia is the foundation of my work and the beginning of my creative process. I want to evoke a mood of tranquility, harmony and meditation upon the subjects I'm exploring. Each painting, finished in miniature, reflects a world of its own."[17]

Quite the opposite of Halili is **Ernest Concepcion**, another comics superhero enthusiast, has from a young age been drawing fantastic scenes. As an adult his works are of mythic mural sizes, completely invented by him. Born in the Philippines after the People Power Movement, he was shielded by his parents from the turmoil in the country and being the youngest sibling, he was left alone at home with a maid while his parents went to work and his brother went to school, a typical middle-class family. The TV became his companion and friend. The *Birth of Ona (Brainyacks A)* (Pl. 10), is an endless fantastic journey that knows no time or logic: a collapsing castle, 20th-century Russian soldiers, a mushrooming atomic bomb, Arabs on Arabian horses watching caravans of barbaric tribes from a mountain, each one occupying his own space in the drawing. Up in the sky are fighter planes in airstrike formation and exploding lava rocks. The sci war narrative goes on and on. On occasion

Fig. 12, *Ernest Concepcion, Gerana (Brainyacks B), 2008, ink, acrylic, colored pencil on paper, 120 x 54 in., courtesy of Ernest Concepcion, Photo Credit: Anthony Louis Rodriguez*

his murals continue beyond the paper and onto the wall when Concepcion is allowed to. His *The Wrath of Gerana* (Fig. 12), a rehash of vernacular *gera na* (war time) a metamorphosing towering figure personifies devastating war wreaking havoc on the world. He says of his process, "A great deal of my drawing process involves losing myself in the process itself…. As soon as I lay down the pen or brush, it's all hell breaking loose. There is a meditative quality on the process that I find very satisfying, and as soon as I finish the work and step back, oftentimes I'm baffled how I ever even did that."[18] This comment could have been an expression of an action painter like Jackson Pollock whose works were dense like Concepcion's, highly textured with incredible movement like Concepcion's, but the final results couldn't be farther apart. What they have in common are the emotions coming into play in the process. Concepcion maintains a figurative expressionist narrative, whereas Pollock maintained an abstract expression.

Buen Calubayan's endless drawing in *Eternal Landscape* (Pl. 11), a graphite on toilet tissue paper at least 50 feet long, depicts the vast Hacienda Luisita farmland of the Cojuanco family in Tarlac, Central Luzon, Philippines. Unlike Concepcion's dense drawing on huge paper, Calubayan's drawing is minimalist in construction, horizontally running lightly by smears of graphite and occasionally textured with dark tree formation on narrow and fragile toilet tissue paper. Whereas Concepcion's theme is invented personal myth, Calubayan's narrative is very real and politically explosive, not only on the issue of land reform but also on the involvement of the Aquino family as part owners.

The Aquinos are respected political figures in the country who have been at the center of political upheaval in 20th-century Philippines. The death of Senator Benigno Aquino Sr. during martial law made him a hero and catalyst to the People Power Movement of 1986. The rise of his wife, Corazon Cojuanco Aquino, to presidency—the Philippine's first woman president—also turned her into a heroine as a champion of compassion for the poor. Current president Benigno Aquino Jr., their son, is being hailed for his watchword "*Daang Matuwid*" (literally straight path, symbolically, incorruptible governance), thus far successful in restoring trust in the government. The Hacienda Luisita farmland has been highly controversial, with questions about the treatment of farmers. Thus, the use of toilet paper satirizes the issue as a low point if not the lowest in upholding human dignity. The Cojuanco family has decided to divide the land among their farmers, and its distribution has started.

Conceptual Art

*I*n the early 21st century, conceptual art has taken root among the new generation of artists. Conceptual art is simply defined as an art form that upholds and totally relies on the concept or idea as the art in itself, dismissing the need for the plastic aspect of art in the process of creation. Unlike all art before it, where the object is the ultimate result of art, in conceptual art the tangible object has temporary existence, its formal content immaterial, and its collectability relying on memory and not on the object. Its common forms are recipes, such as Sol LeWitt's geometric formulas; or recycled objects, ready-mades that acquire different meaning under different environments, such as Marcel Duchamp's famed *Fountain*, which is a recycled men's urinal; or performance art, assemblages, and video art whose physical forms are remembered, recorded or archived, such as Christo's *Gates* 2004 project in New York City's Central Park, lasting a few weeks and now only existing in secondary materials of sketches and floor plans. Mainstream conceptual art evolved in defiance of the commercialization of art, challenging the commercializing effect of collecting for investment.

In the Philippines conceptual art may have stemmed from the use of local materials at the height of social realism, whose primary intent is to develop unique Filipino images. From collages to assemblages, art is farther removed from the painterly process and transformed into more sculptural works, to the total absence of object-oriented art forms like performance art. It did not happen overnight. The transition can be traced in some works in this exhibition.

*R*enan Ortiz's works are a combination of painterly and sculptural processes involving sheets of stencils spray painted on a wall, at times combined with actual objects like toy soldiers. The work, *VerseReverse* (Pl. 12), is an installation that pays homage to literary artist Bienvenido Lumbera's poem "Sila Ang May Hawak ng Baril" (*They Possess the Arms*) and people's lawyer Edre Olalia's legal paper "*The Status of Liberation Movements in International Law*." It is part of a 2011 exhibition entitled *Sprout*, dedicated to the insurgency, peace and initiative for socio-economic reform in the country. *VerseReverse* uses two walls facing each other to simulate a dialogue or an exchange using a huge black painted hand on one wall representing the "haves," and on the other, spray-painted, much smaller hands joined at the center with bullets looking like butterflies as the " have-nots," signifying the continuing battle on land reform in the Philippines. This work is only part of a four-part installation. Other works of the artists are ready-mades, like an assembly of 50 television sets all tuned in one channel, perhaps decrying the dulling effect of technology to humans.

*P*rofessor **Leo Antonio Abaya** seems to be an all-around artist who dabbles with cinema, graphic arts, commercial art, comics and theater. An inventive artist who could not contain his diverse interests, he makes his own statement of Philippine politics set on a huge chess board, with the chess pieces as political figures. Entitled *Rigodon* (Pl. 13), a 2013 interactive installation made of vinyl

"...in conceptual art the tangible object has temporary existence, its formal content immaterial, and its collectability relying on memory and not on the object."

paint, acrylic emulsion and stickers, the stickered chess pieces are positioned presumably by their stance in real politics in the country. A tantalizing title, *Rigodon* is a French folk dance introduced in the Philippines through Spain. Of this work he says,

> I was inspired by the metaphorical possibilities of the chess game as it relates to the idea of the Office of the President of the Philippines. But I didn't fancy the idea of using objects, nor making a painting to push my point. Stickers are uncomplicated to make. The checkerboard pattern…is visually striking…without being spatially obstrusive. That it is on the same level as the floor that viewers walk on creates a kind of tension…. Since I can paint, sculpt, do installation, and make a video, I don't [see] why I should confine myself and specialize in any one of them. For me it's possible to have a voice even in such circumstances.[19]

Controversial conceptual artist **Mideo Cruz's** primary aim in his art is to challenge his viewers to engage in deep thought, which he achieves by juxtaposing opposite realities in his art. "I do like to provoke debates and critical thinking," he explains. "Art is a way of expressing one's views about the world, culture, and history, and this is what I do in my work."[20] Why, one might ask, would an artist spend his time on issues that enrage the society to the point of endangering his life and being called a blasphemous son of Satan? His response is, "Growing from a country in Southeast Asia where we are geographically settled but mentally uncertain, my works usually discuss the ironies of my immediate location and experiences."[21] The statement refers to his use of icons held sacred by society, icons that as time passes take on a

life of their own in a society where the individual's natural ability to assess his own needs are weakened if not stifled. His installation entitled *Politeismo*, which makes reference to idolatry, is a controversial work that he submitted to the 2011 exhibition *Kulo* (boiling point) at the Cultural Center of the Philippines. It caused the indignation of the Roman Catholic Church, Roman Catholic Filipinos (87 percent of the population), and the Filipino-American public. He received threats on his life, and the shutdown of the exhibiting institution was called for. Violent public reaction seems to have been his wish, but the message remains vague.

In the artist's opinion, it is simply to encourage a debate on idolatry. In my opinion, the message is simply to cancel out images or the effects of images to allow the individual to dwell on the value of the matter without the use of an icon or a picture. This not only applies to religious icons but also to celebrities, cults and belief systems that use images to entice people to engage in the matter. This artist further raises his issue to the level of commercialism applied to the subject matter. In this exhibit he demonstrates this once more by obliterating icons, pictures of saints, and Hollywood celebrities.

A similar challenge applies to his work *Untitled* (Pl. 14), a cibachrome photograph of farmers standing in the rice field holding a placard that says "Untitled," referencing two realities in one image—that of the farmers not owning the land they have cultivated for generations, and that of the work itself being labeled as "Untitled." Which one do you see? Get it?

"In the Philippines conceptual art may have stemmed from the use of local materials at the height of social realism."

Christina Quisumbing Ramilo, a returning Filipina from New York, uses sarcasm as well in creating a gigantic one hundred peso bill out of cut-up real money in *Mukhang Pera* (*Like Money*), a 2011 collage. The wit lies in the devalued currency literally made useless with the act of destroying in order to create an illusionistic big currency. The title is a Filipino colloquial expression, heightening the double meaning behind the expression denoting iniquity in sacrificing ethical principles for money. Early works of this artist created while she was in New York displayed angst and nostalgia for her country of birth. Since her return to the Philippines, she has delved into memories of childhood, as in *Dreamtime* (Pl. 15), an altered ready-made recycled basketball ring of iron and cultured pearls as ultimate tribute to her parents—her father whose favorite pastime is basketball, and her mother, whose sewing ability created useful forms and patterns. Ramilo's latest works are fragments and discarded junk gathered together and dignified by the new reality in which they are recreated.

Racquel DeLoyola is a performance artist who carries moralizing messages in her performances. In *Blemish*, preserved in video documentation of performance/installation done in *Blemish (B)* (Pl. 16), she launders clothes, and as she pounds on white sheets, blood gushes out as the names of real people are recited one by one who are victims of violence silenced by the oppressive society. The gut-wrenching scene captured on video challenges the viewer's moral values. DeLoyola says of this work that it is her way of giving the victims voices they didn't have in life and in death.

Mark Salvatus's works are commentaries of urban life. A small-town boy growing up in Lucban, Quezon, he uses his appreciation or perhaps awe of cosmopolitan Manila prominently in his works. The video entitled *Haiku* (PL. 17), a 2012 single-channel video projection of graffiti in the streets of the big city, conveys a glimmer of the fast

life in Manila. Graffiti on building walls is frowned upon as dirt and clutter destroying beautiful urban landscapes. Somehow, presented in the context of a video, which is likened to watching television, the otherwise disgusting scenery not only becomes bearable but interesting pieces of life in the city that capture the emotions of real-life people—anger, joy, desperation, verdicts, curses. Another work depicting over development he entitled *Model City*, (Fig. 13), a 2012 single-channel video projection featuring towering high-rise buildings in all spaces available. "Every day in the Philippines is political," he says, "in the sense that everything around you is connected to something bigger than the individual. I use everyday objects and experiences to present my work in a new context. If presented in a subtle yet humorous manner, these familiar objects or experiences, that are often taken for granted, become think-pieces for issues."[22]

Filipino-American **Mark Orozco Justiniani** presents shrewd, teasing and insightful works nearly all focused on his Filipino childhood experiences. Multi-talented, he is good with the brush and mechanical put-together, inventive with words, and fascinated with double-meaning situations. He loves to mesmerize his viewers with "blink of eye" curiosity, which they call in Pilipino *malikmata*. One of the organizers of *Sanggawa*, he is considered among the best Filipino surrealists, not of the gory kind but one that defies logic, such as in *Balanghay, an early Filipino boat*, where he puts

Fig. 13, Mark Salvatus, *Model City*, 2012, single channel video projection, Image courtesy of the artist and The Drawing Room Contemporary Art Manila & Singapore

many people in a newspaper boat sailing in rough seas. Or, a play on words in "i am God," which in the mirror reads "Dogma!" the beginning "I" in lower case to resemble the exclamation point. His crafty mirror works are manipulated to reflect and refract hundreds of times to create illusions of unfathomable depth, such as *Debris*, (Pl. 18), but the actual work could be only six inches deep. A 1994 13 Modern awardee from the Cultural Center of the Philippines, he has been acknowledged with many other international citations.

The Market

Considering that it was hardly reviewed and rated as folk art in the Western art world less than fifteen years ago, to call Philippine Art triumphant would seem a far cry from reality, particularly in the realm of contemporary art. This claim is, however, supported by developments in the Asian art market and a kind of confirmation of this art in the 21st century. The current art market frenzy in Asia, a phenomenon unto itself, was favorable to Philippine art in the last decade of the 20th century, and the momentum continues in the 21st century. The international auction giants Sotheby's and Christie's have set up bases in Hong Kong and Singapore, where they have Philippine art on their short lists of favorites due to its consistent good performance at the auctions.

In 2007, BenCab sold his small acrylic on paper, **Brown Brother's Burden** for US $54,000 (2.160 million pesos), an astonishing performance way beyond the expected US $19,000 estimate. Anita Magsaysay-Ho amazed the market with her painting, **Banana Vendors**, pegged at US $28,000, sold for US $84,000 (3.360 million pesos), and to Christie's pleasant surprise, Ho's **In the Marketplace** painting fetched US $375,000 up from a $ 10,000 to $15,000 estimate. Astounding too is Felix Resurreccion Hidalgo's **La Parisienne** at US $369,000 (14.760 million pesos). Many other known names in Philippine art—Vicente Manansala (**Jeepney**, US $80,000), Fernando Amorsolo (**A Lady By The Cooking Fire.** 1941, US $41,700), Carlos Francisco, Jose Joya, Romeo Tabuena, Juvenal Sanso, Arturo Luz, Malang Santos, and a succession of younger artists—prove that Philippine art has established its marketability on the auction block. This confidence is likewise reflected in the Western market, with European museum purchases of Philippine modern and contemporary art, such as Nena Saguil's painting sold to a Paris museum for US $67,000 in the mid-1980s[23] Alfonso Angel Osorio, who never had a solo exhibition in the Philippines, is well collected in U.S. museums. Rising Filipino-American artists Paul Pfiffer, Ernest Concepcion, Gregory Raymond Halili, and Mark Justiniani are represented in New York Galleries. It was unthinkable twenty years ago that international artists BenCab, Brenda Fajardo, Imelda Cajipe-Endaya, Julie Lluch, Mark Justiniani, Elmer Borlongan, Mark Salvatus, the late Pacita Abad (the first Asian woman recognized with Excellence Award in year 2000 by the National Museum of Women in the Arts, Smithsonian Institution) and other artists would be traversing the art world with exhibitions. There is now a demand for Philippine art. As Holland Cotter of **The New York Times** reported, America's big museums are shifting their collecting habits towards Asia, Southeast Asia and the Philippines included.[24]

The primary buyers of Philippine art are, however, the new growing upper-middle-class Filipino collectors who have the sophistication to purchase through auction houses, another phenomenon unto itself.[25] Further, a new group of young highly educated Filipinos who are globally oriented, market-savvy entrepreneurs looking into art for investment, compare art to real estate as depreciation risk free, but, unlike real estate, art is transportable and does not have the citizenship requirement with which real estate is saddled. The rate of appreciation is 10 percent yearly and up to 30 percent yearly for the most valuable works,[26] meaning those works that are characterized by name recognition, good execution and great provenance. Filipino imagery could be added to this list. Exhibitions abroad have been avenues and opportunities for wider global exposure afforded to Philippine art by Filipino-American expatriates. They have helped pave the way towards global exposure in countries like Australia, France, the United States and parts of Asia, for example, the *First Asian Pacific Triennial of Contemporary Art*, Queensland Art Gallery, Australia,1993; *Asian Modernism: Diverse Development in Indonesia, The Philippines, and Thailand*, Japan Foundation, 1995; and *Modern and Beyond*, Singapore Art Museum, 1996.

As to what drove this great development, Filipino art critic and former curator of the Ateneo University Art Gallery, Emmanuel Torres, shared his thoughts: internationalism was redefined in the 1980s; the development of the Association of South East Asian Nations (ASEAN) fostered unity in the region; there was a recognition of commonalities among ASEAN member nations marked by the colonial experience; the cultural, ethnic, spiritual, aesthetic and language patterns that brought mutual respect and collaboration in the region are unique subjects to which the world could relate; and the breakup of the Paris/New York hegemony in the arts, a previously tightly Western-influenced art market, has become an advantage for the Asian art market to move forward globally.[27]

For the Philippines this has been a long awaited and much needed development, a spark from a long period of more than 300 years of slump from the colonial period. The 21st century is bright for globally competitive Philippine art. Undoubtedly, the new imagery of Filipino art could be attributed to the transformation that occurred in the country over a period of 50 years. The search for national identity necessitated not only the will of the people but also the support of institutions and the rise of a strong group of collectors, along with a robust Asian art market. Institutional support is manifested under Proclamation No. 1001 of April 27, 1972 to recognize Filipino artistic talent through the National Artists Awards in the fields of music, dance, theater, visual arts, literature, film and broadcast arts, architecture and allied arts to be administered under the guidance of the Cultural Center of the Philippines. The creation of the National Commission on Culture under Republic Act No. 7356 in April 2, 1992, as the agency responsible for the development and promotion of the Filipino national culture and the arts and to award persons who have "significantly contributed to the development and promotion of Philippine culture and the arts."[28] The rise of museums and galleries and collectors also contribute greatly to the robust contemporary art of the Philippines.

Endnotes

[1] Fr. Casal, Gabriel, et al. **The People and Art of the Philippines**, Los Angeles: Museum of Cultural History, University of California, 1981.

[2] Capistrano-Baker, Florina H, et al. **Philippine Ancestral Gold**, Makati City: Ayala Foundation, 2011, p. 37.

[3] Paras-Perez, Rodolfo, **Fernando C. Amorsolo Drawings**, Manila: The Lopez Museum, 1992, p7-8.

[4] Benesa, Leo. "Philippine Contemporary Art as a Post-War Phenomenon," **What is Philippine in Philippine Art?,** Manila: National Commission of Culture and Art, 1975.

[5] PSR is the acronym for the book, **Philippine Social Revolution,** by Jose Maria Sison.

[6] Kolesniknov-Jessop, "The Birth of a Region's Political Art," Opinion, **The New York Times/International Herald Tribune**, Oct. 19, 2006.

[7] Baen Santos, Pablo, Kaisahan manuscript, Manila, 1976.

[8] Reyes, Cid, **Ben Cabrera Etchings: 1970-1980**, Manila: Tito Roy and Francisco Navarro, 1980.

[9] An Ifugao is an inhabitant of the Cordillera mountain in northern Philippines.

[10] Ibid.

[11] Artist's statement, Athena Santos Magcase-Lopez.

[12] Julie Lluch, "The Making of a Feminist," **Yuta: Earthworks by Julie Lluch a Retrospective**, Manila: National Commission For Culture and the Arts, 2008.

[13] Feminist Movement in the Philippines (from wikiPilipinas).

[14] Cajipe-Endaya, Imelda, artist's statement.

[15] **Family Affair: Philippine Political Dynasties**, PhilStar, May 11, 2013 edition.

[16] Gomez, Michael Geronimo Rodriguez, Artist Statement.

[17] Gregory Halili, Artists' House, Phila, PA.

[18] Aranda, Rocio, **Ernest Concepcion**, El Museo LaBienal 2013, **The New York Times**.

[19] Abaya, Leo, artist's statement, 2013.

[20] Silverio, Ina Alleco, "Who is Mideo Cruz and Why are People Baying for His Head?" InterAksyon.com, the online news portal of TV5 (Philippines), Aug. 9, 2011.

[21] Cruz, Mideo, artist's statement, 2013.

[22] Ferrer, Iris. "Re-imaging the Future with Filipino Artist Mark Salvatus—Interview," **Art Radar Asia**, June 30, 2013.

[23] Abad, Pacita. "Investing in Philippine Art," **Philippine Business Magazine**, Vol. 10 No. 2.

[24] Cotter, Holland. "Acquired Tastes of Asian Art," **The New York Times**, Feb. 21, 2012.

[25] Kasilag, Giselle P., **Investing in Philippine Art**, Manila: Art Sentral, Kulay Diwa.

[26] Ibid.

[27] Torres, Emmanuel. "The Pinoy Visual Artists," **Pananaw I**, Manila: National Commission for Culture and the Arts, 1997.

[28] The National Artists of the Philippine Guidelines.

Bibliography

Abad, Pacita, "Investing in Philippine Art," *Philippine Business Magazine*, Vol. 10 No. 2.

Abaya, Leo, artist's statement, 2013.

Aranda, Rocio, *Ernest Concepcion*, "El Museo La Bienal 2013," *The New York Times*, June 14, 2013.

Baen Santos, Pablo, *Kaisahan Declaration of Principles* manuscript, Manila, 1976.

Baerwaldt, Wayne, ed.. *Memories of Over-development: Philippine Diaspora in Contemporary Art*, Canada: University of California, Irvine Art Gallery, 1997.

Benesa, Leo. "Philippine Contemporary Art as a Post-War Phenomenon," *What is Philippine in Philippine Art?*, Manila: National Commission on Culture and the Arts, 1975.

Canete, Reuben Ramas, ed. *Suri Sining: The Art Studies Anthology*, Manila: Art Studies Foundation, Inc., 2011.

Capistrano-Baker, Florina H, et al. *Philippine Ancestral Gold*, Makati City: Ayala Foundation, 2011.

Fr. Casal, Gabriel, et al. *The People and Art of the Philippines*, Los Angeles: Museum of Cultural History, University of California, 1981.

Datuin, Flaudette May V. ed. *Alter/(n)ations: The Art of Imelda Cajipe, Endaya*, Quezon City: University of the Philippines Press, 2010.

Endaya, Imelda Cajipe, ed. *Pananaw 1, Philippine Journal of Visual Art*, Manila: National Commission for Culture and the Arts, 1997.

Cajipe-Endaya, Imelda, artist's statement, 2013.

Cotter, Holland. "Acquired Tastes of Asian Art," *The New York Times*, Feb. 21, 2012.

Cruz, Mideo, artist's statement, 2013.

Family Affair: Philippine Political Dynasties, PhilStar, May 11, 2013 edition.

Ferrer, Iris. "Re-imaging the Future with Filipino Artist Mark Salvatus—Interview," *Art Radar Asia*, June 30, 2013.

Feminist Movement in the Philippines (from wikiPilipinas).

Flores, Patrick. *Brenda Villanueva Fajardo: Lawas, Kalag, Ispiritu*, Pasay City: Cultural Center of the Philippines, 2005.

Flores, Karen Ocampo. *13 Artists Awards 2009*, Pasay City: Cultural Center of the Philippines, 2009.

Friis-Hansen, Dana, et al. *At Home and Abroad: 20 Contemporary Filipino Artists*, San Francisco: Asian Art Museum, 1998.

Halili, Gregory Raymond, Artist Statement, 2013.

Kolesniknov-Jessop, " The Birth of a Region's Political Art," Opinion, *The New York Times/International Herald Tribune*, Oct. 19, 2006.

Kasilag,Giselle P., *Investing in Philippine Art*, Manila: Art Sentral, Kulay Diwa, 2009.

Legaspi-Ramires, Eileen, ed. *Pananaw 7, Philippine Journal of Visual Art*, Manila: National Commission for Culture and the Arts, 2007.

Lluch, Julie. *Yuta: Earthworks by Julie Lluch, A Retrospective*, Pasay City: Cultural Center of the Philippines, 2008.

Lopa, Trickie E., ed. *Art Fair Philippines 2013* Journal, 2013.

Lopez, Santos Magcase, Athena, Artist Statement, 2013.

Paras-Perez, Rodolfo, *Fernando C. Amorsolo Drawings*, Manila: The Lopez Museum, 1992

Reyes, Cid, *Ben Cabrera Etchings: 1970-1980*, Manila: Tito Roy & Francisco Navarro, 1980.

Sta. Maria, Felice and Ruth Roa, eds. *Modang Modern: A Change Begins*, Manila: Metropolitan Museum of Manila, 1990.

Silverio, Ina Alleco, *"Who is Mideo Cruz and Why are People Baying for His Head?"* InterAksyon.com, the online news portal of TV5 (Philippines), Aug. 9, 2011.

Torres, Emmanuel. "The Pinoy Visual Artists," *Pananaw I*, Manila: National Commission for Culture and the Arts, 1997.

EXHIBITION PLATES

PL1
Benedicto Cabrera, *1081*,
1975, etching aquatint,
23 x 21 inches
Collection of the artist

PL2
Pablo Baen Santos,
***Labor and Monkey
Business,*** 2010
Oil on canvas, 72 x 84 in.,
Courtesy of Pablo Baen
Santos

PL3 **ATHENA MAGCASE-LOPEZ**

PL3
Athena Magcase-Lopez,
***Sumungaw Na
Liwanag (A Ray
of Hope),*** 1986,
oil on canvas, 19 x 21 in.,
Courtesy of The Estate
of Melvyn Patrick Lopez

PL4
Julie Lluch,
Philippine Gothic,
1984, ceramic, 1.5 x 2.5 ft.,
Courtesy of Julie Lluch,
Photo Credit: Gari Buenavista

PL5
Brenda Fajardo, ***Baraha ng Buhay Pilipino: Walang Katapusang Naghalo and Balat sa Tinalupan,***
1989, ink on paper, 20.9 x 28.7 in., Courtesy of Maria Lourdes Jacob, *Photo Credit: Rolando Codes*

PL6
Imelda Cajipe Endaya,
Inay, Ineng, Kalayaan
ay Inyo Rin,
1985, oil and collage on
canvas, sawali mounted on
wood, 72 x 96.1 in.

PL7
Karen Ocampo Flores, **A Line of History**, 2008, mixed media (collage, acrylic, oil) on canvas, 38 x 72 in.,
Courtesy of Karen Ocampo Flores, *Photo Credit: Rolando Codes*

PL8
Michael Geronimo R. Gomez,
Duplicity Multiplicity,
2013, mixed (polymer clay,
wood, terra cotta clay,
cement, paper), 11 x 8 ½ x 8
½ in., (two views) Courtesy of
Michael Geronimo R. Gomez

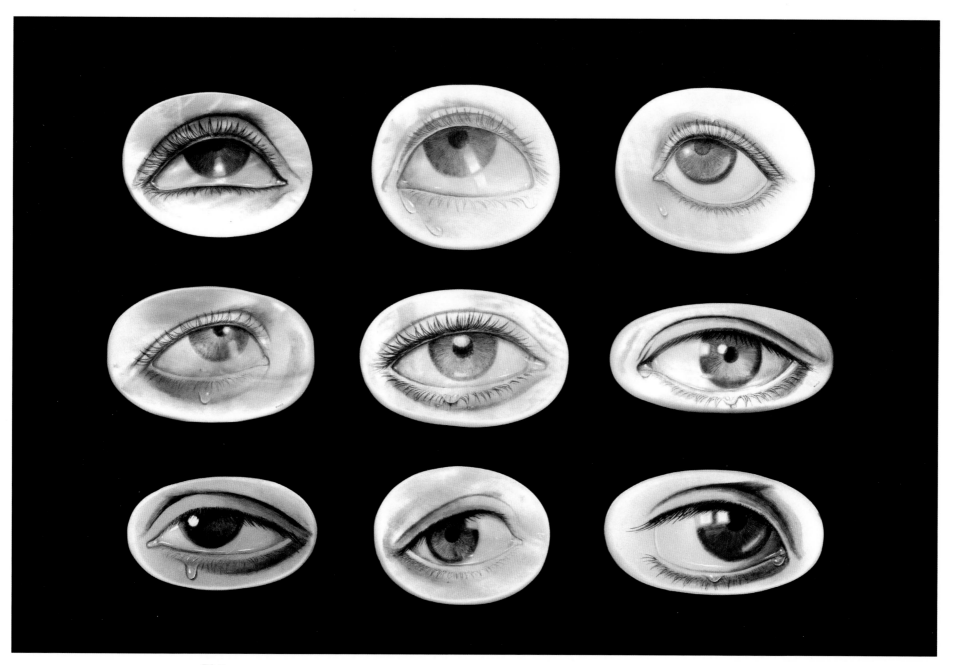

PL9
Gregory Raymond Halili, ***Sorrow,*** 2013, mother of pearl, 9.25 x 12 in., Collection of Lynda and Stewart Resnick

PL10
Ernest Concepcion,
***The Birth of Ona
(Brainyacks A)***,
2006, ink, graphite, colored
pencil on paper, 72 x 144 in.,
Courtesy of Ernest
Concepcion, *Photo Credit:*
Anthony Louis Rodriguez

PL11
Buen Calubayan,
Eternal Landscape,
2010-2013, graphite and
charcoal on tissue paper,
4 x approx. 463 in., Norman
Crisologo Collection

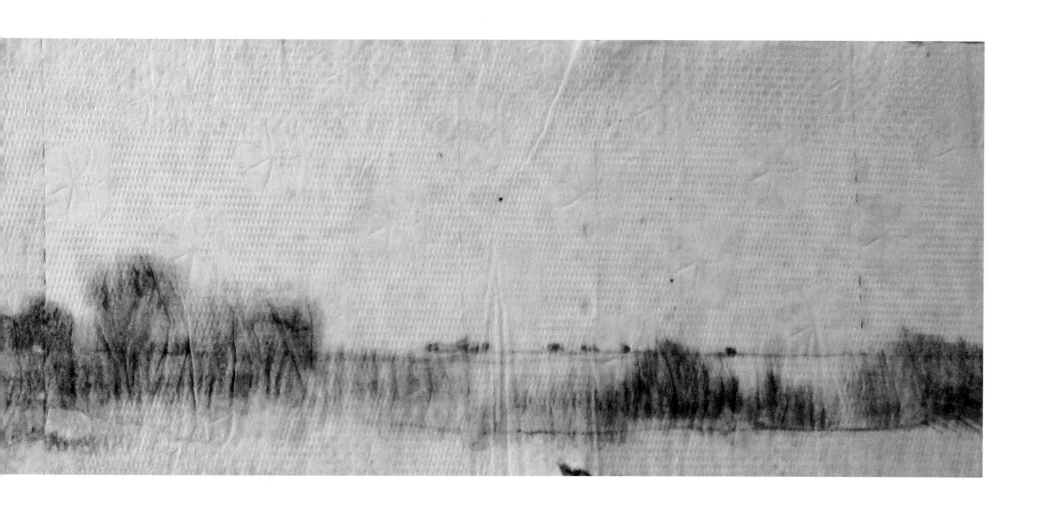

PL12
Renan Ortiz,
VerseReverse, 2011,
drawings on wall, 96 x 144 in.,
Collection of the artist

PL13
Leo Abaya, *Rigodon,* 2012, vinyl, paint, acrylic emulsion and stickers, 144 x 144 in.,
Courtesy of Leo Abaya, *Photo Credit: Marya Demigillo-Salang of Tin-aw Art Gallery*

PL14
Mideo Cruz, **_Untitled (A)_**, 2012, C-print monoprint, 28 ½ x 40 in., Courtesy of Mideo M. Cruz

PL15
Christina Quisumbing Ramilo,
Dreamtime,
2010, basketball ring and fresh
water pearls, 18 x 18 x 25 in.,
Courtesy of the Artist

PL16
Racquel De Loyola, **Blemish** (video documentation of a performance/installation), 2009, video monitor, found cloth, found plastic hanger, AP, Courtesy of Racquel De Loyola

PL17
Mark Salvatus,
Haiku,
2012, single channel projection/video,
Image courtesy of the artist and The
Drawing Room Contemporary Art
Manila & Singapore

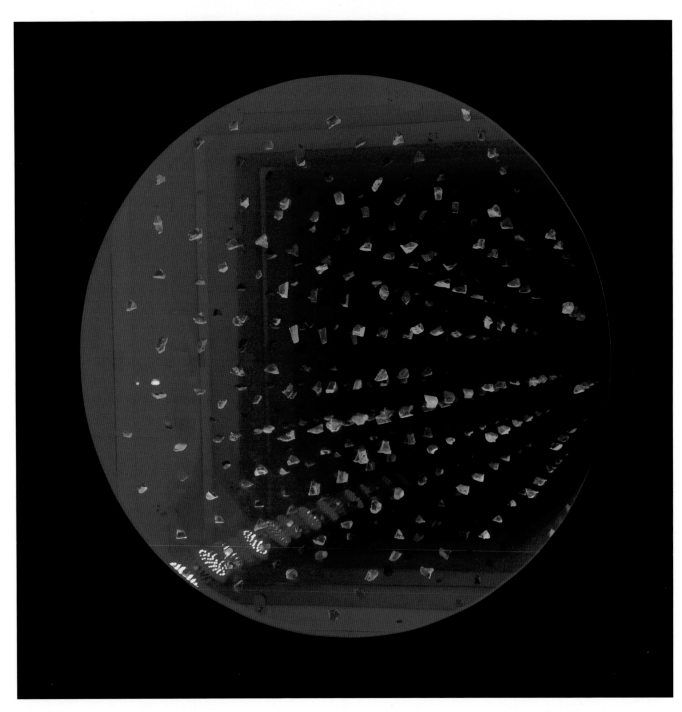

PL18
Mark Orozco Justiniani, ***Debris***, 2013, reflective media, lighting fixtures, wood, and objects. 24 x 24 x 6.25 in., Courtesy of Tin-aw Art Gallery, *Photo Credit: Tin-aw Art Gallery*

EXHIBITION CHECKLIST

EXHIBITION CHECKLIST

1. Leo Abaya
Rigodon
2012
vinyl, paint, acrylic
emulsion and stickers
144 x 144 inches.
Courtesy of Leo Abaya
Photo Credit: Marya
Demigillo-Salang of
Tin-aw Art Gallery

2. Benedicto Cabrera
1081
1975, etching aquatint
23 x 21 inches
Collection of the artist

3. Benedicto Cabrera
Marlboro Country
1975 etching aquatint
23 x 21 inches
Collection of the artist

4. Benedicto Cabrera
From Hillman to Sargeant
1978
3-color plate etching
21 x 24 inches
Collection of the artist

5. Benedicto Cabrera
O.T. in Chicago
1978
2-color plate etching
29 x 25 inches
Collection of the artist

6. Buen Calubayan
Eternal Landscape
2010-2013
graphite and charcoal on
tissue paper
4 x approx.463 inches.
Norman Crisologo
Collection

7. Mideo Cruz
Untitled (A)
2012
C-print monoprint
28 ½ x 40 inches
Courtesy of Mideo M. Cruz

8. Mideo Cruz
Untitled (B)
2012
C-print monoprint
28 ½ x 40 inches
Courtesy of Mideo M. Cruz

9. Mideo Cruz
Postcards (altered group
of religious images)
(28 pcs.), 2013
acrylic, Industrial paint,
stencil on postcard
9 x 11 inches
Courtesy of Mideo M.
Cruz

10. Ernest Concepcion
*The Birth of Ona
(Brainyacks A)*
2006
ink, graphite, colored
pencil on paper
72 x 144 inches
Courtesy of Ernest
Concepcion
Photo Credit: Anthony
Louis Rodriguez

11. Ernest Concepcion
Gerana (Brainyacks B)
2008
ink, acrylic, colored
pencil on paper
120 x 54 inches
Courtesy of Ernest
Concepcion
Photo Credit: Anthony
Louis Rodriguez

12. Imelda Cajipe Endaya:
Bintana ni Momoy
(4 pieces), 1983
48 x 74 inches
Ateneo de Manila
University Art Gallery
Collection

13. Imelda Cajipe Endaya
*Inay, Ineng, Kalayaan ay
Inyo Rin*
1985
oil & collage on canvas,
sawali mounted on wood
72 x 96.1 inches
University of the
Philippines Bulwagan ng
Dangal Collection

14. Brenda Fajardo
*Baraha ng Buhay
Pilipino: Walang
Katapusang Naglaho and
Balat sa Tinalupan*
1989
ink on paper
20.9 x 28.7 inches
Courtesy of Maria
Lourdes Jacob
Photo Credit: Rolando
Codes

15. Brenda Fajardo
Tarot Card Series: 6
Acrylic on paper
21 x 28 inches
Collection of Ninotchka
Rosca. Photo Credit:
Anthony Louis Rodriguez

16. Brenda Fajardo
Tarot Card Series 7
Acrylic on paper
21 x 28 inches
Collection of Ninotchka
Rosca. Photo Credit:
Anthony Louis Rodriguez

17. Karen Ocampo Flores
A Line of History
2008
mixed media (collage,
acrylic, oil) on canvas
38 x 72 inches
Courtesy of Karen
Ocampo Flores
Photo Credit: Rolando
Codes

18. Michael Geronimo R.
Gomez
Duplicity Multiplicity
2013, mixed (polymer
clay,wood, terra cotta
clay, cement paper)
11 x 8 ½ x 8 ½ inches
Courtesy of Michael
Geronimo R. Gomez

19. Michael Geronimo R.
Gomez
Botokabajan
2012, mixed (polymer
clay, wood, terra cotta
clay, cement, paper)
8 x 5 x 5 inches
Courtesy of Michael
Geronimo R. Gomez

20. Gregory Raymond Halili
Sorrow
2013
mother of pearl
9.25 x 12 inches
Collection of Lynda &
Stewart Resnick

21. Gregory Raymond Halili
Sorrow II
2013
mother of pearl
9 x 30 inches
Courtesy of Gregory
Raymond Halili

22. Gregory Raymond Halili
Constellation XI
2007
watercolor on paper
10 x 10 inches
Courtesy of Gregory
Raymond Halili

23. Gregory Raymond Halili
Constellation XII
2007
watercolor on paper
10 x 10 inches
Courtesy of Gregory
Raymond Halili

24. Gregory Raymond Halili
Celebration in Blue XI
2013
watercolor on paper
10 x 10 inches
Courtesy of Gregory
Raymond Halili

25. Gregory Raymond Halili
Celebration in Blue XII
2012
watercolor on paper
10 x 10 inches
Courtesy of Gregory
Raymond Halili

26. Mark Orozco Justiniani
Debris
2013
reflective media, lighting
fixtures, wood, and
objects
24 x 24 x 6.25 inches
Courtesy of Tin-aw Art
Gallery, Photo Credit:
Tin-aw Art Gallery

27. Julie Lluch
Philippine Gothic
1984
Ceramic
1.5 x 2.5 ft.
Courtesy of Julie Lluch
Photo Credit: Gari
Buenavista

28. Athena Magcase-Lopez
**Awit Ng Isang Ina (Song
of the Motherland)**
1986
oil on canvas
30 x 46 inches
Courtesy of The Estate of
Melvyn Patrick Lopez

29. Athena Magcase-Lopez
**Sumungaw Na Liwanag
(A Ray of Hope)**
1986
oil on canvas
19 x 21 inches
Courtesy of The Estate of
Melvyn Patrick Lopez

30. Racquel De Loyola
Blemish (video,
documentation of a
performance/ installation)
video monitor, found
cloth, found plastic
hanger, AP
Courtesy of Racquel
De Loyola

31. Racquel De Loyola
Blemish (A) (photograph
documentation of a
performance/ installation)
2009
Giclee on paper, AP
20 ½ x 28 ½ inches
Courtesy of Racquel
De Loyola

32. Racquel De Loyola
Blemish (B) (photograph
documentation of a
performance/ installation)
2009
Giclee on paper, AP
20 ½ x 28 ½ inches
Courtesy of Racquel
De Loyola

33. Renan Ortiz
VerseReverse
2011
drawings on wall
96 x 144 inches
Collection of the artist

34. Christina
Quisumbing Ramilo
Mukhang Pera
Currency, mirror, wood
18 x 38 x 1.5 inches
Photo Credit: Anthony
Louis Rodriguez

35. Christina
Quisumbing Ramilo
Dreamtime
2010
basketball ring
fresh water pearls
18 x 18 x 25 inches

36. Mark Salvatus
Model City
2012
single channel video
projection
Image courtesy of the
artist and The Drawing
Room Contemporary Art
Manila & Singapore

37. Mark Salvatus
Haiku
2012
single channel projection
/video
Image courtesy of the
artist and The Drawing
Room Contemporary Art
Manila & Singapore

38. Pablo Baen Santos
**Labor and Monkey
Business**
2010
oil on canvas
72 x 84 inches
Courtesy of Pablo
Baen Santos

APPENDIX

Kaisahan (Solidarity) Declaration of Principles

We, the artists of KAISAHAN, commit ourselves to the search for national identity.

We believe that national identity is not to be found in a nostalgic love of the past or an idealized view of our traditions and our history. It cannot be achieved by using the common symbols of our national experience without understanding the reality that lies within them. We recognize that national identity, if it is to be more than lip service or an excuse for personal status seeking, should be firmly based on the present social realities and a critical assessment of our historical past so that we may trace the roots of these realities.

We shall therefore develop an art that reflects the true conditions and problems in our society.
This means, first of all, that we must break away from the western-oriented culture that tends to maintain the Filipino people's dependence on foreign tastes and foreign ways that are incompatible with their genuine interests. We reject this culture in so far as it perpetuates values, habits and attitudes that do not serve the people's welfare, but draw from it whatever is useful to their actual needs. We shall therefore move away from the uncritical acceptance of western models, from the slavish imitation of western forms that have no connection to our national life, from the preoccupation with western trends that do not reflect the process of our development.

We realize that our search will be meaningless [if] it does not become a collective experience, an experience that is understood by the broadest number of people. In its beginning, art was not the isolated act that it is now: it was as necessary, as integral, a part of the people's lives as the knowledge of when to plant.

For us therefore, the question "for whom is art?" is a crucial and significant one. And our experiences lead us the answer that art is for the masses. It must not exist simply for the pleasure of the few who can afford it. It must not degenerate into the pastime of the few cultists.

We are aware if the contradictions that confront us in committing ourselves to this task. At present, under the conditions of our times, the audience who will view our works will mostly be the intellectuals, students, professionals *and others who go to the galleries. But we wish to gradually transform our art into an art that has a form understandable to the masses and a content that is relevant to their lives. At present, it is inevitable that our art is sometimes commercialized. But we should use this [as] a means and not as an end for our artistic expressions.*

Our commitments to these objectives need not mean that we limit ourselves to a specific form or a specific style. We may take different roads in the forms that we evolve and use but we all converge on the same objectives. The only limitation to our experimentations, to the play of our creative impulses is the need to effectively communicate social realities to our chosen audiences.

To be true works of the imagination, our works of art should not only reflect our perceptions of what is, but also our insight into what is to be. We grasp the direction in which they are changing, and imagine the shape of the future. We shall therefore develop an art that not only depicts the life of the Filipino people but also seeks to uplift their condition. We shall develop an art that enables them to see the essence, the patterns behind the scattered phenomena and experience of our times. We shall develop an art that shows them the unity of their interest and thus leads them to unite.

We issue this declaration of principles, knowing that today, it is not considered fashionable for artists to be serious to have ideas and to commit themselves to something more than their own personal pursuit of fame.

Therefore, we do not hope to find much favor among those who use art merely to decorate their walls or to escape from the barrenness of their existence. It is our hope that our works of art should more than anything else, endure and that the spirit of our times should live on in them and reach other generations.

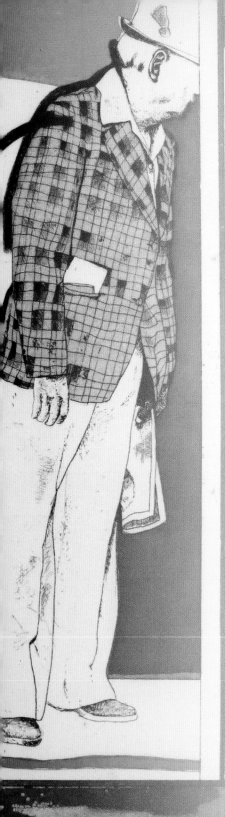

EDUCATIONAL PROGRAMS

- **Online Streaming: Montclair to Manila,**
  Live Dialogue with the Artists
  September 25, 2013
  9 a.m.

- **English in the Philippines:**
  Burden or Benediction
  Luis Francia, speaker
  October 10, 2013
  6 p.m.

- **Triumph of Philippine Art**
  M.Teresa Lapid Rodriguez, speaker
  October 17, 2013
  6 p.m.

- **The Colonial Roots of Violence Against**
  Women in the Philippines
  Ninotchka Rosca, speaker
  October 24, 2013
  6 p.m.

- **A Triumphant Future: Filipino American**
  Youth Forum
  Produced in cooperation with MUFASA
  and Zeny Almario
  December 4, 2013
  6 p.m.

Detail from Benedicto Cabrera
O.T. in Chicago, 1978

- **Filipina Feminism and Sexuality**
  Dr. Jorshinelle Taleon-Sonza, speaker
  December 5, 2013
  6 p.m.

- **Musical Journey: Struggles for Cultural Identity**
  Philippine Chamber Rondalla of New Jersey
  December 7, 2013
  1:30 p.m.

- **Classic Filipino Piano Scores**
  Played by Reynaldo Reyes
  November 17, 2013
  2 p.m.

Detail from Athena Magcase-Lopez
Awit Ng Isang Ina (Song of the
Motherland), 1986

SPONSORS

 New Jersey State Council on the Arts

This exhibition was made possible in part by funding from the New Jersey State Council on the Arts/Department of State, a partner agency of the National Endowment for the Arts.

John McMullen Family Foundation

 The Philippine Consulate General, New York

 Ayala Museum

University of the Philippines Alumni Association-New Jersey, Inc.

Norbert and Elizabeth Wirsching

V.C. Igarta Arts Center

Advent Consulting Associates, Inc.

Tess Aguilar

Rolly Almario

Millenia of Philippine Art

Fil-Am Pag-Asa Club of UMDNJ

Del Gow

Maureen Promin

Cora Crisostomo Tolentino

Myrna Sangil Vergara

LENDERS

Ateneo de Manila University Art Gallery
Ayala Museum
Bulwagan ng Dangal, University of the Philippines
The Drawing Room Contemporary Art Manila and Singapore
The Estate of Melvyn Patrick Lopez
Tin-Aw Art Gallery

Leo Abaya
Benedicto "BenCab" Cabrera
Norman Crisologo
Mideo Cruz
Ernest Concepcion
Karen Ocampo Flores
Michael Geronimo Rodriguez Gomez
Gregory Raymond Halili
Maria Lourdes Jacob
Julie Lluch
Racquel de Loyola
Renan Ortiz
Christina Quisumbing Ramilo
Lynda and Stewart Resnick
Ninotchka Rosca
Pablo Baen Santos
Paulino Que

GEORGE SEGAL GALLERY

George Segal, ***Woman Painting Her Toenails,*** plaster, painted wood, painted glass, 1996